RISE
OF THE
TRUST FALL

BY MINDY NETTIFEE

A Write Bloody Book
Long Beach. CA USA

Rise of the Trust Fall
by Mindy Nettifee

Write Bloody Publishing ©2010.
2nd printing.
Printed in USA

Rise of the Trust Fall Copyright 2010.
All Rights Reserved.

Published by Write Bloody Publishing.

Printed in Long Beach, CA USA.

Cover Designed by Joshua Grieve
Interior Layout by Lea C. Deschenes
Edited by Derrick Brown, shea M gauer, Saadia Byram, Michael Sarnowsk,
        Cristin O'Keefe Aptowicz
Proofread by Jennifer Roach
Type set in Helvetica Neue and Bell MT

To contact the author, send an email to writebloody@gmail.com

WRITE BLOODY PUBLISHING
LONG BEACH, CA

"All growth is a leap in the dark."

—Henry Miller

RISE OF THE TRUST FALL

III.

AFTER WE SAW KIDS POINTING AT THAT DEAD BABY WHALE ON THE BEACH DURING THE MOST ROMANTIC SUNSET EVER AND YOU SAID "I GET IT" ALL BITTERLY AND I SAID "I'M NOT SURE YOU DO"

Now that Joni Mitchell lyrics have started to make sense to you.
Now that your beard is no longer a fashion statement,
but a crude three-dimensional graph illustrating
the number of years you pictured her lips while failing her.
Now that you've cried so hard and long the 4th Street
beggars are pressing quarters into your palms.

You know how good it can feel, in its own way,
to be so profoundly disappointed in yourself.
How strangely magnificent, to be this demolished,
to have taken it, as they say, like a man—on the chin, to the testicles—
to have tried to take a bite with your last dangling tooth of dignity
and come away starving and grinning and sobbing.

'Cause really, how much worse can it get?
Short answer: a lot worse.
Don't think about that right now.
You've broken all the promises you never made,
and few that you did, and they turned around
and broke you right back.
So be it.

From here on out you don't have to pretend
to be perfect, or whole, or even right.
Your eyes can take a vacation
from being windows to your soul.
You can hang out with the other war torn countries,

who you suddenly share a language with.
Poland will show you her scars.
Croatia will teach you card games so cutthroat
you won't be able to speak for days.
Iraq will start accepting your apologies.

It may not feel like it just yet
but you've stumbled upon a kind of freedom.

Your stomach now full of pride,
you can take your expectations off like clothes.
Stand outside in the cool night air
and show off your brand new shamelessness.
Howl if that's your thing.
Scare the neighbor's cat.
Breathe easy.
Notice the Moon's gained weight.

TREMOLO

When my father began selling off his things,
he put off unloading the Steinway baby grand piano
as long as possible, and had the decency to call me
when it was time. He was practiced at postponing disaster.
The piano was the highest ticket item he had. I knew
how badly he needed the money, so, it meant something.

The sign of a great piano is how quietly you can play it
is what he told me when he bought it, when he was
at the summit of his happiness and self-philanthropy.
He had this gleam in his eye back then, when he was
entertaining guests, that I mistook for joy. He would
brandish the glossy black back of it like a pet whale, like

an endangered species he had become close friends with.
He would be sure to point out where Henry Z. Steinway,
great grandson of the patriarch himself, had signed it,
just inside the haughty curve of its hip. What is hubris,
anyway, if not the signal of great imagination? Of someone
who has let the true self float up like a hot air balloon?

What would you jettison to stay in the soft bright clouds
just one more day? At the time, I was still in love
with my father the way children are. The dark
growth of his mistakes was weighing everything
down now, and I wanted his weakness to bring out
something gentle in me. Even though I had learned

the *Pathetique* on this piano. Even though I had
scaled its fingers with my fingers nearly every day
for seven years. Even though I could close my eyes

15

while seated at any table, see the keys take their positions
like skinny dancers on a chess board, and play the blank wood
perfectly. I told him, "It's okay, Dad. It's just a thing,"

then placed the phone back in its cradle, my eyes burning,
my hands shaking, my heart hammering out the song
that isn't a dirge, but how a dirge begins in the mind
of the composer, when she is still trying to get a handle
on the shape of it, the swelling changing shape
of the loss.

ACCEPTANCE SPEECH

I would like to thank first of all my asthmatic lungs,
my inadequacy in the bedroom,
my dark Texas reckless streak and waning night vision
that make awareness of my own mortality possible.

Next, I would like to thank my constant nightmares
for their vivid, arresting creativity—
their cheerful execution of ritual disembowelment,
their lifelike rendering of flesh-eating animatronic bunnies,
and their resourcefulness in general with symbols for personal failure.

I must thank my inability to balance a checkbook
coupled with my whimsical attitude about money
and my magically disappearing work ethic,
without which my debt would be nothing.

And while we're at it, thank you Blockbuster Video
for ruining my credit with $17 in late fees from 1996.

Next: a big thanks to my father, the pathological liar
who, in his way, taught me to be a poet.
Thank you sanity for being a finite natural resource.

To my crippling self doubt: thanks.
To my weak left eye, my squishy arms,
my smaller right breast, misshapen as a Tijuana coin purse: thanks.

Thank you allergic rash.
Thank you pens which run out of ink when I'm finally being brilliant.
Thank you humiliation, with a special shout out to Brad Carlson.*

Thank you to my guts.
I love your red twistyness, your endless judgmental bullshit,
your fleshy gears, your broken alarm bells
that look like little French knots.
I trusted you.

Finally, I would like to thank you
for sleeping with that other woman
who was so much prettier than me.
For a moment, you really had me going—
whip cream puppies, slippery cloud sex, forever and ever and all that.
There was so much sweet hope in my plastic farm heart,
the ants were building sugarcastles in my ventricles.
There was so much dopamine sogging my brain
I thought we had invented flying.

It's so much better here on the ground,
where the morning light tastes like asphalt and swing set rust.
Where everything has teeth that glow.
Where I can afford large grains of salt
with the money I save
buying into nothing.

* *Brad Carlson you know what you did.*

WHAT YOU SAW

They say if one hundred people were witnesses to the shoot out
there will be one hundred different versions of what happened
that day. One hundred and two if you count the shooters,
which you do, and one hundred and four if you count the guns,

which you don't, not yet. If you gather all these stories
and weave them together, you will come as close as you
can come to seeing what God sees. But the weaving is tricky.
You have to memorize the angles of sight. You have to interview

each witness separately and learn their life story. Why did
witness #35 assume the first shooter started the whole thing?
Did he look like the brother she lost? Did the other shooter blink
or did she blink, when the clouds sifted and the sun flashed briefly?

Each telling will be a cumulative telling of a thousand other stories.
It would be best if you could start at the beginning, talk to the
families of the witnesses in their childhood homes. Their first lovers.
It would be better still if you could teach all of them to play the piano,

record and analyze how they approach Beethoven's sonatas,
or the blues of Memphis Slim. The way music pours out of you,
it's a form of lie detector test, if there was no such thing as lying.
Time itself is another angle, distorting everything. If you want to

get to the whole truth, just keep layering dimension upon dimension.
Undo the tapestry when it gets tangled and start over. Use string and
feathers and whatever clocks you have on hand. They say every writer
has only one story to tell, and they tell it over and over and over,

trying to get it right. Or not right—perfect, the way God would tell it,
if God came out of the cage of your body long enough to draw breath
and sing. Maybe that's why I'm still sitting here, in this growing
mountain of paper, furiously taking down accounts. I don't need
the notes anymore. It's only important that I take them, because

I learn through writing things down. For example: I'm writing,
"Don't forget to ask the guns. Important ***." Now I'll remember
for sure. Tomorrow morning, I'll shovel a tunnel through the stacks
of pages and start to work getting the perspectives of objects.

I could just start a fire; burn the stories to create a pathway out.
It would be easy. But then there would be all that smoke.
It would obscure the whole scene. I might miss the final,
most crucial detail, the one ties this all together with one
big
    bang.

WHEN THE ECONOMY WAS BOOMING

We used to masturbate to Radiohead
or slide in some Nine Inch Nails and hook
our thumbs around the jutting hip bones
of some skinny messy boy.

The world was ours enough at least to piss
and puke and fuck on. We repeated favorite mistakes
like solid gold records, spun our wheels in thrift store
stilettos, dotted vanilla extract on our wrists.

We erased the muscle memories of our mothers
by cooking recipes for homemade bombs.
We spoke only in famous last words.
We were free in the only way we knew how.

Nihilist joy whores. Kids kicking up sand.
Railing scowling Neo-Marxist darlings. The earth
we knew was made of crushed shoe box caskets
and chalk lines and the hot dust we all turn to.

You have to make your own sense. Fear wants all
or none of you, so become the bad element. Beat 'em to the punch.
It will always be dangerous to be a girl, to be anything so soft.
Better to carry a lit cigarette. Spike your charm bracelets.

Walk with a death wish so strong
the Santa Ana dogs whine your song.
Better to control the lighting you'll be objectified in,
even if it's dark.
Even if you can't see anything at all.

I HATE THAT PATTERN

Every woman's closet is a museum of her insecurities.
Also, in fairness, her unique assortment of sensory processing disorders.

Rule #1: don't look at what is there.
Look at what isn't.

Rule #2: don't ever ask a woman why she wears all that make-up:
it's like asking a complete stranger
why she never buried the hatchet with her father before he died,
in a room full of her co-workers,
on Christmas Eve.

Unless of course you want to see her not-cry.
Unless you want to see her not-cry so hard
her entire body turns to stone.

There are other rules, but I don't get to know them yet.
My closet is filled with vintage coats it's never cold enough to wear.
Stick that in your Jung pipe.

My mother's face is sage with intricate loss and the abiding of it.
There are happiness secrets fugitive in the lines around her eyes.
She performs a daily regimen of facial exercises
to make her face look more youthful.
I think women with the souls of alligators invented them.

In her closet, the number of exotic blouses
is indirectly proportional to the number of Friday nights
she's had hot dates.

I look at all that sad sequin beaded detailing,
and I turn to tell her, no—remind her—how extraordinarily
mind-blowingly beautiful she is.

But it's just like when she would tell me
when I was twelve and lonely and scowling at mirrors,
using her most powerful earnest-mom-eye-lasers,
that I was really beautiful.

I knew how much she loved me.
I didn't believe a word.

AND YOU CAN KISS YOUR
HAND-EYE COORDINATION GOODBYE TOO

"The gunmen were well-prepared, even carrying large bags of almonds to keep up their energy during the fight."
—from "Forces Assault Besieged Jewish center In Mumbai", Huffington Post, Nov. 27, 2008.

This was my point exactly, when we were ten minutes late leaving
because I had to stop and pack almonds and an apple and water,
and you were yelling at me because you hate being late.

Sometimes you have to be your own mother, or Scoutmaster,
or terrorist force coordinator. You need to take the extra ten minutes
to plan and stock up on supplies, think through contingencies.

Otherwise there you are, four hours into the biggest siege of your life
or 45 minutes into evangelical church services, adrenaline filling
all the swimming pools in your eyes, and your blood sugar starts to drop.

BAM!—there goes your good mood.
There goes months of training and rehearsal and preparation,
not to mention the lifetime of repressed-then-channeled rage

it took to get here, built up like a personal generator in your gut.
There goes your rational mind, which should be patiently sharp shooting
or scanning environs to map exit strategies,

but is instead dedicated to staving off tears of frustration,
to picturing the assistant pastor as roast turkey with fixings,
the goal of the entire revolution now, lunch and a nap.

IN OUR BEDROOM, BEFORE THE WAR

In the morning light
soft shoeing through the Venetian blinds
we blink our sleepy faces into focus
and begin the quiet memorizing
of pillow creases and eye jam,
filling all the secret pages
of the encyclopedia of us.

You ask me for the hundredth time
if I'll marry you already,
without really asking.

I've gotten used to you adoring me,
to that look on your face
when I give you exactly what you want.

Later, I won't know how to say
what I'm about to say to you.
I'll be avoiding your eyes and eating, like,
twelve sour candies at once,
the opposing surfaces of my mouth
going Cuban missile crisis
from the combined emergency
of tartness and fear of rejection.

But right now, in all this earliness,
I just want you to push the red buttons of my lips
with the red buttons of your lips.

You can't help but laugh at my eyebrows collapsing,
at my face crushing with disappointment
when the upstairs neighbors start the shower
and begin playing the Eagles "Hotel California" on repeat. LOUD.

When you laugh, I laugh.
We don't smell any ocean breeze.
We don't feel the earth turning beneath us.
A cat crouches on the fence
outside the bedroom window,
perfectly silent, perfectly tensed,
its whole weight now on the hinges of its hind legs,
ready to spring.

TO THE BEST THING THAT EVER HAPPENED TO ME

I am writing you from an eight foot snow drift
somewhere south of somewhere.

I would call, but I lost my cell phone two days ago
at the ice rink pity party that was really just me,
a frozen lake, some cheap Russian vodka and
a depressed polar bear. (Those guys are dark.)

I still have six waterproof matches
and what Vogue Magazine assures me
is twenty extra pounds of body fat.
No, I am not proud of myself.
No, I am not done with my "obsession with Survivalism."

But I am sorry. I am sorry we fought.

You were right when you said writing poetry is not a real skill
applicable post-apocalypse, and I said but who will tell the good stories,
and you said guys who can fish with their bare hands.

It turns out that's really hard.
Trout are ticklish,
and my hands do not have to do what I tell them to.
Some sort of freezing cold water clause.

I have nothing but the time and space I've been pining for now,
and I am using this opportunity to try and remember
why I thought this was a good idea.

I think it had something to do with escape,
which has permanent offices in the romance division of my brain
and ground troops in my solar plexus.

The flight instinct comes on quicksand,
muscles out all rational thought,
starts Morse coding my limbic system with
complex dots and dashes for strange verbs that mean,
roughly translated: "joyous chewing your leash off,"
and "fire without readiness or aim."

It always feels so right to go,
like it's the only story my body knows by heart:
the creation myth of Alaskan shorebirds,
the bedtime story highways whisper to dirt roads,
the real reason horses sometimes obey.
You really wanted to marry me, didn't you?

My eyelashes are soaked now.
I'm beginning to think I will never see you again,
that I will never see anything again
but the twenty yards or so of visibility
in stark panorama around my broken sled.
I feel like an idiot, but I'm not scared.
You'd think I would be scared.

These are the soft frozen fields tundra vacations too,
the great white quiet.
No one to distrust.
I deserve this.
You would be amazed how much light there is.
The stars stay out all night.
Each snowflake is a mirror.

PSUEDO-HAIKUS READ BETWEEN THE LINES OF THE ASTROLOGICAL BIRTHDAY GUIDE THAT SAYS I HAVE THE SAME BIRTHDAY AS MALCOLM X, JOEY RAMONE AND GRACE JONES

No pressure. Really.
We just thought you should know
what you're capable of.

In theory of course.
Astrologically speaking.
Just what the stars say.

You and your excuses
will always be more powerful
than nuclear reactions.

No matter how inspiring
the poets make them sound—
they are only gas;

burning, luminous orbs
scattered across the universe
inventing radiance

maybe, but just gas.
No one expects anything from you.
Go pour another.

ALL I HAVE TO SAY FOR MYSELF

The last time you came to see me
there were anchors in your eyes,
hardback books in your posture.
You were the five star general of sureness,
a crisp, white tuxedo of a man.

I was fiddling with my worn coat pockets,
puffing false confidence ghosts in the cold January air.
My hands were shitty champagne flutes
brimming with cheap merlot.
I couldn't touch you without ruining you,
so I didn't touch you at all.

Its when you're on the brink of something
that you lose your balance.
When I can't bring myself to say what I need to,
my heart plays Russian Roulette with my throat.
I swear I fired that night, but, *nothing*.

Someday, I'll show you the bullet I had for you,
after time has done the wash.
I'll take it out of the jar of missed opportunities.
We'll hold it up to the light.
You'll roll it around your mouth like a fallen tooth.
We'll laugh about how small it is,
wonder how such a little thing
could have meant so much to anyone.

THE THINGS I CAN NOT FIX GET TOGETHER FOR THEIR ANNUAL REUNION CAMP OUT

They are so excited to see each other!
They immediately get out the coolers of overpriced foreign beer
and toast to being out of my control.

Everyone brings toy guitars and broken tambourines,
and each night they gather around the fire to dance
and hold hands and sing all the classic Things-I-Can-Not-Fix camp songs
such as "My Sister Votes Republican," and "Pollution Related Cancers"
and that sweet reverse protest number "White Male Entitlement, Ooh
     Ahh Ahh."

I must say, this year's altar to my mistakes is breathtaking.
Who brought the glitter candles shaped like all the stages of an eating disorder?
They look amazing on top of that half-burned bridal corset.
And the empty bottles of lubricant I sold to all those lawyers
and wetland developers the year I worked at the sex shop?
The way they're glued to cracked bike helmets like little junkyard mohawks?
Genius.

You should go next year. I really think you'd love it.
No one prepares for turns in the weather.
No one packs batteries for the flashlights.
But there's plenty of firewood, plenty of kindling and matches;
plenty of marshmallows shaped like the dumb dreams of children,
ready to be stabbed with sticks.

ILL-ADVISED BAND NAMES THAT ALSO ILLUSTRATE MY LAST FIVE BREAK-UPS

Moral Outrage

Mediocre Sex Jams

Mall Security All-Stars

Whiskey Night Sweats

Decoding Nostradamus

YOUR NEW GIRLFRIEND IS REALLY NICE

You are an impossible birthday party.
You are cloud climbing.
You are muscle relaxant archery.

I was never a straight shooter with you,
so I'm telling you now
while I've got this strange bravery messing my chest:

I love you like Mexican wrestlers love their outfits.
I miss you like graffiti misses clarity.
I want to crack open for you like a sinner on Sunday.

When I see you kiss another woman
my arm hairs form armies of Elliott Smiths
sifting the wind for some soft suicide song.

You're the naughty punctuation mark I've always been looking for.
You're the electric chair that completes my sentence,
the starving wolverine in my mailbag of wholesome thoughts.

I am afraid of regrets. In my dreams they rise up
like froth mouthed horses, apocalypse black and freaking out.
When I'm awake, I can trick myself into believing almost anything.
It's not magic; it's serial optimism.
But I'm not buying our someday.

Your gravity is moonshine. It's not the real dance
of two heavenly bodies, or even the bumping of two cake forks
at the dessert table. I just wanted to let you know I know.

I just wanted to warn you, I'm signing up for vanishing lessons.
if I ask to you to meet me on a windy pier somewhere
overlooking the sandy blue cash of the Pacific,
if I ask you to wear your best wool coat,
don't show.

MOON SHOT EXHIBIT ROOM
AT THE JFK LIBRARY

From this close, the Project Mercury space suits hanging
in the center of their glass museum apartment
look like unworn children's party costumes.
The prototype assembly drawings lack some gravitas as well.
They could be early sketches for jet packs, or the colored pencil
architectural blueprints you did when you were nine,
for the castle you were going to build overlooking the cliff
of your bunk bed. The space helmets could be advanced
paper-mâché, the playful taxidermied heads of astronauts.

But at this point in the presidential library,
at least six swelling JFK speeches in,
I am prepared to believe just about anything.
His voice has a quality I am unprepared for in longer stretches.
When he talks about the American character,
about our fixed regard for principle,
I can smell my first brand new social studies textbook.
I can remember this old feeling, a surge of effortless pride
at my young, sunburned, wide-eyed Americanness.

When he says we should choose to do things
because they are hard, I practically raise my own taxes.
Just think – there was a time when we believed we could
conquer poverty and racism, crush the black heart of Communism
and travel to the moon if we were just organized enough,
if we just marshaled our resources in the directions of our better dreams.
All of this makes the coming exhibits especially hard to take.
On twelve monitors, Walter Cronkite is choking up,

the quickening pulse of the newsroom and the tight held breath
of an entire nation straining the scene. The confusion and chaos
of what's next swirls and eddies, and does not settle.
I want to go back to the Moon Shot room. I want to go back
and stare at the artifacts, at those treasure maps to pipe dreams.
But it wouldn't be the same.

There's this chunk of the moon on display there,
suspended in a clear thermoplastic pyramid.
The plaque says it is more than three-billion years old.
Three-billion: it sounds like a made-up number. But I know it's not.
I know that long, exponential springs of time are behind all the
        quickest leaps.
That what I can see in the sky at night
might already be gone,
even though the shouting of the stars is so clear, so bright.

ULTRA VIOLET

Amanda's recurring dream as a child was about a witch and a bathtub
and how hard it is, really, to strangle someone with your own bare hands.
Never mind that the choked witch was her self, her own power.
She wouldn't know that for years, anyway, and until then she had to fall
asleep terrified each night and wake up sick with victory.
Until then she had work to do, to become beautiful and worthy.

We praise all who come out of hiding to claim their lease on the sun.
We reward pride in all its forms, throw parades for it so we can liberate
flowers from the straightjackets of our fists and call it Spring.
We don't talk enough about the difficulty of staying in the closet,
of disowning the only part of you that knows how to say your name.
What it takes to keep the struggling color of you quiet and reined,

when it was born to scream and river—it is an incredible feat of hesitation
to live with your hands around your own neck and smile about it.
What fierce love we have for our mothers and fathers
that we go to such lengths to return their protection.
Someday you will have your parade, Amanda, I have no doubt.
You will have streamers every color of every rainbow and the whole world

barely containing their pleasure at your pleasure, their shared joy
just zippered behind the warm closed ellipses of their lips.
But this one is for the little girl in the bathtub, preparing to fight.
I suspect she knows something about survival.   You do what you have to,
live pinned beneath floorboards , crouched in attic closets.
You imagine every crumb is a wedding cake.

Guard closely what is most precious, and wait out the war.
Hold your breath when you hear another horn section warming up outside.
Shine the lock on the door. No one can tell you how to write your own story

but I will tell you a secret: *the witch can not be killed.*
We are so limited by the spectrum of what is visible.
How many things are dazzling in the dark? Are secretly thriving
just out of sight?

II.

IN MEDIAS RES

That summer, all the kids started taking peyote and forming drum circles.
At first, there was a new light in everyone's cheeks,
like their very souls had been saturated with molten honey answers.
The meaning of life hung over us like a golden disco ball,
like a sun you could stare into forever and not go blind.
We wandered around the town hugging strangers
and everything we said sounded like Alan Watts had said it first,
and no one was ever hungry or scared or alone.

The clouds cried long shadowy tears in the middle of August.
It didn't ruin the Weekend Ganesh Jam or the Leftovers Cook-Off one bit.
When your eyes are dilated snake-coins-of-the-one-true-vision
everything is exactly as it should be.
We danced in the rain and washed our parents' sarcasm off our skin,
and didn't feel reckless at all. We danced like it was our last chance
to control what we would become, to force something holy to happen to us.

I think that's when the nightmares started.
I can't speak for what anyone else saw, but what I saw was this:
a long corridor lined with dark grey business suits swaying,
one for each day of the rest of my life.
I curled up next to a pair of stiff shoes and cried.
The entire universe creaked like a ship in the middle
of a churning ocean, and my bones ached with the knowing
that none of us could ever go home again.

We'd gone looking for the Sacred Untouched Garden of Pure Intentions,
and we found it with the gate kicked in, ivy strangling the azaleas,
and a stoned guardian who'd shirked his duties to practice
pissing messages in perfect cursive into the river.
That's how everyone talked about it afterward anyway—

in long parable metaphor chains that were both vague and specific
and drove the adults to complicated sounding hybrid mood stabilizers.

Nobody got hurt or anything, thank God,
unless you count the rash of Celtic knot tattoos
and the spike in herpes transmission. Fall was a real drag.
Everyone hallucinated patterns in their breakfast cereal
and a real air of apocalypse hung over the town.
Fights broke out at the high school over the definition of anarchy.
The Mayor died suddenly of a secret
even his wife hadn't known.

There was no ominous fog. No steady post-war drizzle.
No great storm. October came, then November.
The Hendersons won the pumpkin contest
at the county fair for the fifth year running.
The leaves blushed and yellowed and gave up, one by one,
until the trees were so bare, you could see clearly into everyone's houses.

HOW TO GET UNDER MY SKIN

First off, you can stop looking for the zippers.
I hid those long ago, when my two sisters
and twelve-year-old boys everywhere
made rather athletic headway exploiting my soft spots,
disguising insults as compliments I wouldn't discover
until later, in therapy, like bummer cracker jack prizes.

Get subtle.
Start with how much you love orangesicles.
Start with jokes about Egon Schiele and pedophilia.
Start with lame stories from summer camp,
your first awkward salty kiss.

Nostalgia is anesthesia.
I am gripped by how soft you remember humiliation—
that summer you were grounded.
How you mapped the route out of that house,
that town,
that promise.

There are small openings everywhere:
the last time you saw your mother,
how you picture her sleepless nights on your sleepless nights.
How you save your best punch lines.
Bust one out for me.
I'll weaken like a nurse in a massage chair.
I won't notice I'm tearing up.

Lean in and smell my shampoo.
Let it get dark.
I go down when you figure out how close I came

just by looking me in the eye,
when we compare childish suicide attempts with hot sauce and aspirin.
I go down when you cast shadows on my shadows,
when it doesn't scare you
that I don't know how to flinch.

THE BENT KINETICS OF MEMORY

In trying to explain how to measure
the trajectory of an object tossed into space
or the effect of spin on flight
or the momentum equations of collisions,
my physics teacher Mr. Russell always turned to baseball.
Drawing tiny arrows of meaning on a chalkboard
to illustrate some home run parabola,
he would be transported in his own personal baseball time machine.
He would eyes-closed grin like we were all there with him.
Like the sun was shining and the beer was free.
Like we could picture it *exactly*.

He lost me immediately.
It wasn't his teaching style,
or the obviousness with which he favored the boys,
or even his obsession with the acoustics of wooden bats.
I had only just begun writing,
but already, I was entering the world through stories,
through the curious mechanics of narrative and connection.
My lack of concentration had nothing at all to do with Mr. Russell
and everything to do with the fact that in the baseball file in my brain
it was and will always be the summer of 1988:

the year my mother moved my sisters and I back to California;
the year I started refusing socks and cursing secretly;
the year I came home from the fourth grade in tears
because the kids had been playing AIDS tag in the school yard.
It was just like normal tag, except the "It" kid was "a gay."
One slight touch to the arm or back meant you were now gay, too,
and had AIDS, which meant instant death, an actual location
beside the kindergarten water fountains.

It was the year I started to square with my intuition
that evil was airborne, that it spread through what you said aloud.
And it was the year my little sister fell in love with Orel Hershiser,
who pitched 59 consecutive scoreless innings,
pissing off Don Dreysdale and any batter worth his salt,
taking the Dodgers to a World Championship that produced
so much pure joy in the city of Los Angeles battered wives got flowers;
men laid off from factories felt their hearts charge with hope;
new kids at school could don shiny royal blue Dodgers jackets and belong.

"Don't drop the ball!" Mr. Russell would say and laugh to himself,
while passing out quizzes on Magnus force or passionately arguing
that Babe Ruth could most definitely have hit Sandy Koufax.
I would be time-traveling a reverse chronology of a year—
the first time I snuck out of our cramped one bedroom apartment
to walk to the ocean and watch the moon arch its back light
across the hazy dark; the time my sister caught me
using her Mike Scioscia rookie card as a book mark
in a Nancy Drew novel and disowned me for three weeks.

When I should have been learning the practical applications
of force and speed and distance and power,
I was stuck in the wine colored upholstery of a 1982 Ford Fairmont
watching the corn golden fields of Iowa slip stream past
as my mother ran toward her boyfriend,
toward the Pacific Ocean,
away from her mother,
away from safe harbor of her hometown,
toward some freedom she could only imagine
and not yet understand,
three small daughters
and an empty bank account be damned.

MULTICULTURALISM

I. Raised By Gays

Made physically ill by most fabric patterns.
Automatically catalogues hardware and window treatments
by presence, absence, type and astrological sign.
Can poach, blanche, and parboil.
Can identify five different shades of Versace gold.
Suspicious of authority.
Suspicious of men who drive white trucks.
Suspicious of women with bad perms.
Suspicious of anyone who needs permission.

II. Raised By Liberal Hippie Christians In the 80's

Has dreams about a large blue hymnal named Psalty the Psalm Book.
These are not sexual dreams.
(Maybe they are.)
Becomes suddenly restless and angry upon hearing the word "vespers."
Accused by Catholic boys of being "too principled." Also: "a slut."
Brain wired by Jim Henson.

III. Raised By Women Who Read And Clipped Newspaper Articles

Has heard the words out of her own mother's mouth:
You know there are alternatives to penetration, right?

IV. Raised By Iowans

Understands the verb "shuck" and how to perform it.
Can smell storms coming.
Smiles at strangers with frightening warmth.

V. Raised By Long Beach, California

Has memorized the lyrics to Dr. Dre's The Chronic 2001.
Mistakenly assumes all cops have something better to do.
Harbors secret belief that fog can be controlled with the mind.

VI. Raised By Poets

Can casually quote George Orwell to Republicans.
Considers vocabulary an abdominal muscle.
Enforces honesty as a right, not a privilege.
Describes weather on a scale of Prozac to Shakespeare.
Loves desperately.
Loves like the soul is in the mouth.
Like the mouth is a God factory.
Like entire temples can be built from tiny frozen moments of joy.

FOUNTAINS OF YOUTH REVISITED

Pee-ing In My Snowsuit Fountain
(Griswold, IA)

Bike Gets Stolen And Now You're Walking To School Fountain
(Louisville, KY)

Armpit Besting Fountain
(Sioux Falls, SD)

Comparing My Shitty Science Project To The Rich Kids' Ones Fountain
(Mercer, IL)

First Time I Called My Mother The B Word Fountain
(Springfield, MN)

Noxzema Makes Me Breakout Fountain
(Madison, WI)

Won The Dance Off And Now No One Will Talk To Me Fountain
(Tempe, AZ)

I Don't Give A Care Fountain
(Bend, OR)

Really Bad Short Hair Cut The Week Before School Starts Fountain
(Ashville, NC)

It's Called Unrequited Love Get Used To It Fountain
(Tazewell, VA)

GRAPE JUICE IS THE SWEETEST JUICE!

All preachers' daughters know this.
After small lifetimes
of tasting it doled out in thimbles,
after pretending to understand it
as some sort of stand-in for pre-crucifixion toasting,
some faux wine hired to re-enact savior blood,

all it takes is the hottest day of the summer,
in an old church thick with mildewed hymn books.

All it takes is the Mildreds and the Rubies
and the Irenes to turn their backs long enough
for you to slip through the swinging kitchen door.

If you can get to the fridge door unnoticed.
If you can use your entire body weight to pull open the door,
its rubber seal sticking with Sunday school popsicles and ancient Tang.

If you can unscrew the lid without dropping it:

one big swig
from the Welch's grape juice glass bottle
will make your head swim,

will teach you things about holiness,
they didn't want you to know.

THE DANGERS OF LEAVING THE MIDWEST

My grandmother's greatest fear in 1988
was that an earthquake would come
and California would crack off the Americas
like crust from bread. It would then drift out to sea,
a cartoon ice floe situation, really, but with the
dramatic choreography of an opening act
for the Rapture: the ocean boiling, tidal waves
arching and curling their sinister water claws,
entire families and their puppies being claimed
for the dark underneath.

I studied the matter very seriously.
I drew color coded pictures with maps and arrows
to demonstrate clearly that the plates of the earth
would move north and south along the fault lines.
That if anything, we would end up in Mexico,
which is also California, or the other way around,
which is a national secret (shh!)

She looked like she was going to be sick.
Or like she would slap me, hard,
if it weren't for the arthritis, and her knee jerk love for me,
and the heavy magnet bracelets weighing down her wrists,
and the ten thousand indignities of growing older.
"Esta buena abuelita. It always is," I offered,
and neither of us understood what I said.

SAYING ONE THING,
AND MEANING YOUR MOTHER

I'm having that dream again,
the one where I'm trapped on a tropical island alone
with none of my top five favorite anythings,
writing letters in the wet sand:

Dear Pacific Ocean,
I'm bored.
Please flash me the unseen colors of your Mariana Trench gems.
Please wash up an old game of Boggle or something.

Dear Pacific Ocean,
I'm hungry, and I'm sick of coconuts.
Send a floating crate of bananas this way,
if you're not too busy.

Dear Pacific Ocean,
Tell me more about the lungs of whales.

Dear Pacific Ocean,
I want to learn how to be so vast sailors get lost in me.

No one ever comes to my rescue.
Usually it all just dissolves into some other dream,
like the one where I'm wandering a bombed-out shopping mall,
or knifing my 3rd grade teacher for her apples,
or catering a dinner party where everyone toasts in Freudian slips
and the truth leaves rude red wine stains on everything I love.

But not tonight.
Tonight the stranding is permanent as willful ignorance.
I tire of sitting on the shore.
I tire of never getting letters back.
I try to force myself awake,
like a marionette posing for the wind.
I turn inward and walk to the center of the island,
kill time following the glisten of snail trails.
I hum night carols with the insects.
I weave palm fronds into a giant nutshell
and crawl inside to sleep.
I pray for morning.

RARE CHARACTER ARCS THAT HAVE STARTED TO HAUNT ME

Girl from broken family falls in love, has to learn to trust again, does, passes her dysfunction onto her children anyway, several of whom develop anxiety disorders.

Woman discovers her repressed ambition, works her ass off, battles to break into the boy's club, makes it, learns to live with loneliness and men explaining things to her.

Starving artist goes to law school, discovers money isn't everything, but it beats $2 burritos every night, takes up Paxil and kayaking.

Man confronts profound doubt about the origins of the universe/ existence of God, struggles, eventually retreats in to the simple joys of young adult fiction.

Writer digs deep to express emotions, heal old wounds, still ends up in decades of therapy, dies in her sleep while dreaming about office work.

WHY I SOUNDED SO FREAKED OUT WHEN I CALLED

The newsman's voice makes your own chords jealous.
He reports headlines crisply, hint-of-cheer,
with a tone that encourages, connotes the way scotch
first-love-sexes your chest and lights hearth fires in your throat.
He still manages to convey officiousness, gravitas. It's a gift.

I only listen to the radio when in my car,
and I only get the news from listening to the radio.
Sometimes I go days without being informed.
Sometimes I let the newsman's voice slipstream through me
without really listening to it, and I imagine tiny magical
insects, like half-bee and half-angel-fish, are buzzing
or lightning swimming my neural pathways,
filing all he says away in large gray metal cabinets
labeled "For Conversational Lulls" and "For Future Déjà-Vu."

Being a poet is a degenerative brain-disease.
This electric-crackling insect thing is a perfect example.

Today is a slipstream day, but then—I hear it.
"Rapes are down 14%."
Why don't we have more words for "hear"?
I have to pull the car over.
I put it in park, reach for the passenger side door handle
push the door open and stretch my self across the car just in time.

"Rapes are down 14%."

There are triggers everywhere.
There are springs waiting to loose.
My mouth tastes like stomach acid.
My face is shame flushed.

Yesterday, I was reading *The History Of Love.*
I read, "Perhaps that is what it means to be a father—
to teach your child to live without you."
And like that, there was an explosion behind my eyes,
in the place before where tears form. It set off other explosions,
in all the places in my body I hide. I cried for hours.

Triggers everywhere.
My mouth is so sour.
I think I can feel my tooth enamel decaying.
I think that's what's decaying.

I don't think it's post traumatic stress if there's no "post."
Clearly I have issues. I could come up with a metaphor
for just how many, but I don't feel like cheapening it today.
I could draw you a map of the minefields inside me,
but it wouldn't be a very good map.
The things that will kill me
are as hidden from me as God.

It would be, instead,
a brief history of everything that has happened suddenly,
drawn from an aerial view, from the weather balloon
where the small part of me that isn't Me watches it all.
That blue Rorschach splotch in between houses that looks like half a bird
is the time I was attacked in an alleyway.
That greenish-yellow bruise in the southwest corner
is the time my father phoned to tell me he was about to kill himself.

I am still in my car.
I am really proud that I pulled over,
that I didn't puke everywhere just because of some news headline.
10 Feminist Points. 15½ Adulthood Points.

I pulled over—it's the kind of detail that will never make it to the map,
so I have to hold on to it differently.
The insects will know what to do.
I should be proud that I can feel any of this,
but that won't come for years, if ever.
I'll have to fake that part.

The newsman's voice has moved on to other topics,
but I'm not listening.
My brain is running its programming,
its process for returning me to homeostasis.
My brain is amazing.

Programming cycle 1: Intellectualize
Are they only counting reported rapes?
Are they extrapolating the data?
What number is it that went down 14%?
How many women? How many men? How many children?
How many rapists?
If it's a gang rape, does that only count as one rape?
Is the chief of police celebrating? Is someone getting a raise?

Programming cycle 2: Sort Through All Advice And Possible Applications
First self-defense instructor:
"Stun and run, ladies. If you get taken to a second location,
you are 6 times more likely to be killed."
Second self-defense instructor:
"It's better to be paranoid than dead."
Third self-defense instructor:
"There are two kinds of men, Mindy—
domesticated dogs and predatory wolves.
I'm going to teach you to survive the wolves."
First therapist:
"It's called a panic attack. It won't kill you. Remember it won't kill you."

Programming cycle 3: Poetic Distortion of Reality
Television News can both plant and pull five triggers every 60 seconds.
Porn, seven.
There should be an epidemic of seizures, but there isn't.
How come we say "brain-washing" but never "brain dirty-ing"?

The afternoon sun is making rainbows on my dashboard.
A school bell rings in the distance.
I am collapsing, snapping back into place as each detail registers.

How fucked up,
to be humans living with these animal instincts.
To be animals living with a conscience.
To have the most necessary parts of me made of glass.

The car engine is still running, whirring.

Maybe it's true.
Maybe less men took off the domesticated dog mask this year.
Maybe the men I know aren't wearing masks.
Maybe they love me.
Maybe I'm safe.

My pulse is decelerating, 140 BPM, 136 BPM, 128 BPM.

Maybe I can drive now.

When I get home, I pull up the welcome mat.
I lock the doors.
I pick up the phone.

DISCIPLE

The best advice I ever got about how to heal
came from a beleaguered camp counselor
who found herself suddenly surrounded
by a flock of heaving, sobbing twelve-year-old girls.
It had been billed as a session on conflict resolution,
an alternative to wood cookie crafts, or horseshoes,
and maybe she should have seen it coming,
how water seeks the cracks in any dam.

One girl had been brutally sexually assaulted
by the preschool director, and had not slept
through the night alone since.
One had been molested by her foster brother,
who sliced his arms with scissors in the bedroom dark.
One had been strangled by her own mother,
who later found God and apologized,
and then punished her for not offering up

the fish and loaves of her forgiveness instantly,
the forgiveness which her mother had been promised
by some pastor that she deserved now, and would receive
through the mysterious machines of grace;
the kind that multiplied and magnified and
fed the endless hunger at the center of things.
There were other stories.
Abuse is a word that sounds powerful in your head

and goes limp the moment you speak it,
hanging like a soaked wet curtain
around the things we can not bear to know.
I don't remember the counselor's name, or

what she looked like, just that she was an enormous
buoy of a woman. That her voice was deep
and calm and quavered at all the right turns.
That she sat in a way that trained gravity.

How unprepared she must have felt,
to see the sharks swimming in our eyes,
to have been handed the heavy anchors
of our trust. What well of strength did she draw from?
What inheritance of bedrock and granite and spine?
What gospel stolen from the bent melted steel of kitchen knives?
She absorbed every blow of every word.
When we had finished, when we were softened

by confession, she took a breath and began.
Without getting into the kind of details that get attention,
she told us the story of her own early ruin,
of the lifetimes of gentle obligation it left in its wake.
The heart and the mind and the body
might never align on the requirements of joy.
The mind must be taught patience with the heart.
The heart must learn faith from the body.

The body must be tended lovingly and unwaveringly, an infant.
The heart will take its own sweet time, and can not be rushed.
"Just fake it 'til you feel it," she told us,
and like that, gave us permission
to put on the tight masks of adulthood,
to build walls around what was
too tender and shocked;
to survive.

CRYING AT THE AQUARIUM
for R.M.

I.
It's almost closing time
so we're practically alone.

We're being swallowed
by the spectral sapphire glow of the Catalina Island exhibit.
The waviness of the light, it makes us sick like kids.
We press our palms against the cool glass.

Holiness has always made us dizzy.

We don't make eye contact.
We know.
We're stealing their sanctuary.

Giant kelp sways like naughty skirts, like mute sirens.
Sea stars queen-fuck mollusks.
You hum something by Joy Division.

Then—and no one believes this part—the garibaldi
start actually gathering around to stare back at us.
They whirl into some kind of worship formation and wait.

Your eyes blaze.
You look at me like holyfuckareyouseeingthis?
I want to French kiss hard these fish for making you look like that.

II.
It's deep December.
My father is giving a sermon to his cellmates today
on rebirth, on the promise of the Christ child.

I want to crash LA County Men's Central Jail
and shake the religion out of him,
snap the umbilical Jesus cords and last ropes,
show the communion wafers for the imposters they are.

Your father is somewhere fending off responsibility
for everything he never did for you.
He's got beery kisses and store-bought apologies
all wrapped up in shitty 99 cent Santa paper.

Seasonal redemption for all.

III.
Dear garibaldi:

You are the orange my heart would be
if it got to choose.

You make sunsets bleed with jealousy.

Thank you for making those fucking sea anemones blush.
They're always showing off like park avenue brooches,
like $10,000 pussy.

But you—you gorgeous bitches,
you make Christmas ornaments look like jewelry on corpses.

It's over between me and the scorpion fish.
I'm saving whatever remains of romance for you,
because whatever you gave me,
I can never give back.

AFTER THE FUNERAL

I can't tell if I'm hungry or just empty.
The floor boards won't creak.
There's no bottle of stolen scotch on the mantle.
The Elmore James records won't ache like they used to.
There's no spirit of Charles Bukowski stenching up the place,
no cats in the alleyway, mawing.

There should be.
There's no cinema in this.

I miss cigarettes.
It's just me and my ugliness now.
The two-day-old wine will have to do.

Someday, I want to erect a museum to the world's worst ministers,
the ones who downward spiral drone,
who get increasingly boring the closer they get to their point.
We'll line up stuttering seven-year-olds still learning to read
in the main exhibit hall. We'll dress them in itchy vestments
and have them recite the most moving passages of the Bible aloud.

I'll name the audience participation cringe-o-meter after you.

The minister that performed your funeral told me you are with Jesus now.
That if I don't find Jesus, wherever he is hiding, I'll never see you again.
I know I'll never see you again.
It's not killing me. It's just digging slow graves in my heart.
I hate when ministers mix their anthropomorphic metaphors,
when they confuse mourning with porousness.

This wine tastes like battery acid, with strong berry notes,
and a fuck you finish.
Its sour bitchiness is so familiar it's like drinking a mirror.

Wow. And I'm not even drunk yet.
My mother is probably right.
I shouldn't be alone.
I don't know if I believe in ghosts,
but I can picture them, so what's the difference?

I'm picturing you now, some grey cloud of you,
pulled everywhere that remembering creates anchors.
You're counting crocodile tears,
able to see clearly now, finally,
but still collecting evidence to prove it,
the schizophrenia having shaped you even after death.

You're watching us, memorizing the details of our grief—
your wife's skeletal figure, bent over the toilet.
Your father staring daggers into the walls.
Your mother digging a fat finger in the prescription bottle.

You want to wrap each detail in paper.
You want to keep it, but you don't know how.
You grow more desperate as we grow less desperate.
You try to memorize faster, pulling at our sadness like a kite on its string,
even as what's left of your mind starts to dissipate,

even as your soul form evaporates,
at first softly, then violently,
like white hair chopping in the wind.

MODERN MAGIC SPELLS FOR TROUBLED WOMEN

*For anyone who has ever had to fill out or help someone fill out
a DV100 temporary restraining order request, and felt more helpless
than you've ever felt in your whole life.*

I.

Come on chemicals!
Get out the oxytocin leashes.
Tame the lions at the entrance of the amygdala.
Strangle her cortisol parasols.
Wake the girl out of her niceness trance.

Bring on the moaning tribal hormone lovers!
On dopamine! Fuck yeah serotonin!
Fill her with peaceful rage.
Weave her DNA in the steel plaits of a warrior.
Rush her sinuses with dangerous clarity.
Shush her prayers with mother loads of estrogen.

Come on chemicals, you magic fuckers,
do your worst another day.
Rewire her fuse box.
Turn on the lights.

II.

Sometimes talking to you is like dating emergency
glass I can't break through.

I know you're scared.
He's built mansions of adrenaline in your eyes.
He's marketing his sickness to your blood,
landscaping your heart with dense hedges of scars.
He's turned your nerves to violins
playing out a high strung symphony of
all the ways he could hurt you.

You could lose everything.
You will lose everything.
You're losing everything—

it's the paralysis chorus.
You fog instead of thinking, cloud instead of speaking.
You protect him. It cracks fault lines in your spine,
pools thick grey shadows where your imagination
used to hold previews of your bright Technicolor future.

III.
You are not crazy.
No one ever taught you how this orchestration of instincts works;
how your impulses, they lie;
how quietly your parents' patterns design your choices.
I'm teaching you now.

Finding the right words to say is not a lost cause.
It is THE lost cause.
I want these words to swell your synapses to billionaire hot air balloons.
I want them to open up English channels in your plasma membranes
so I can plant second chances in your cells.
I want these words to unravel your twisted pros and cons,
to untangle your stomach's knots.

Then I want you to stand behind me.
Borrow my brash mouth.
Put on my foolish skin.
Walk into that house waving a pistol
made of all my explosive ridiculous sass and scream,
"Put down your bullshit and no one gets hurt!"

IV.
It is the body that is genius, not the mind.
Magicians are just wordsmiths feeling especially passionate.

Like in those dreams where you speak French even though you don't,
you will wake up one day and speak disaster
like you'd been living there your whole life.
When that happens, you can pull over onto my shoulders.

I will race to the scene of your breakdown like blood to a cut.
I will bring pictures of who you were before all this.
I will hold your hand.
I will hold your hand until you remember
you never needed me at all.

FACT ABOUT GEODES

1.

Geodes generally range in diameter from 1 to 12 inches, though some as large as trees have been reported. Their stomachs are caverns lined with quartz teeth, the fattest, prettiest knives you'll ever see.

2.

Geodes crave salt.

3.

Geodes are born as hiding places: a bubble in cooling volcanic rock, an animal burrow, the pocket left by a tree root, once swollen with nutrients, now just a fist punch in the bedrock. Geodes are second cousins to wombs.

4.

When I discovered my grandfather Harvey's diamond tooth saw, I believed without being told that we were Midwestern royalty. The first time my grandmother Irene used it to cut open a geode for me, I gasped and felt a sharp pain in my left knee.

5.

If stars are very old light, geodes are very old water. It takes thousands of years for minerals from groundwater seep in and harden, layer after layer, creating elaborate labyrinths for light.

6.

Irene loved Harvey, but she was married once before him to a man she loved like you can only love when you're young: epic escapist love, the Houdini of emotions. She divorced him at her parents insistence when the gusts of the Dust Bowl subsided, an obedience as foreign to me as foot binding.

7.

Summer days in Griswold, Iowa blazed inferno kilns. The suns rays had fever claws. Things to do when you're a kid in Griswold on a holy hot day:

—Sweat through Vacation Bible School.
—Memorize the books of the bible.
—Buy a candy bar from the corner store and try to eat it before it melts.
—Play hide and go seek with nobody.
—Go geode hunting by the creek.

I only ever went to Griswold in the summer. I believed it was the center of the earth. I believed four feet beneath my feet was molten god core.

8.

When it got so hot the thermometer stopped reading the temperature, my grandmother got mean. She shouted "ornery" like a broken horn. She made burdens out of us. She told stories to the wall paper about Harvey's mistress, about how her mother refused to name her. It sounded like cackling, like a laugh that has waited in the dark for a hundred years.

9.

When my grandmother died, she was buried on a hill without any shade trees. My mother cried so hard all the rivers dried up. There was a tri-state drought. New deserts were discovered south of Omaha.

10.

When your back is turned, geodes turn inside out. Like diamond porcupines. The most beautiful thing you've ever seen. If they let you see them, it means they want you to touch them. They want to cut your hand.

SATURN RETURN

When the shaking begins, you can't be sure you're not just drunk.
You inventory your bloodstream for vodka stores
while half dreaming of some birthstone mistake
you were just barely grasping in your sleep.
When the quaking gets more violent, when you're sure
that it's happening, you make your way carefully
to the door frame and strike some hieroglyphic pose.

The music of ceramic dishes in the kitchen is gaining momentum.
You're picturing church bells throwing themselves off buildings,
biblical scholars with horse fetishes swooning.
What did your mother say yesterday on the phone?
Are there any batteries in the flashlights?

Other things are falling now: the figurines from that Greek island.
The photographs from someone else's trip to France.
There goes the bottle of pregnant butter Chardonnay you left
on the counter. You can hear it rolling back and forth,
the message of its contents glugging out onto the tile.
There goes the "don't worry so much" of the first sip.
The "everything is going to be okay" of the second glass.

Somewhere outside windows are starting to shatter.
Car alarms are singing the collective panic of a radius of cities.
An odd calm is filling you, some ancient disaster circuitry.
All the things you've been wondering, all that savory
indecision isn't so much eased as erased.
In the dream some part of your brain is still having,
a you-shaped fire being is taking your place,
burning through all that unnecessary shit.

What's left are the sharp teeth of clarity, the bracing.
Change is constant. Resistance can't last.
Eventually, some rigid muscle of rock deep in the thigh of a mountain range
will break under the pressure, will take the whole place with it.
It's what you're feeling now, what's been radiating up into your chest.
It's what's knocking loose inside you, as you finally wake up fully,
as the neighbor's baby starts to cry.

KILL THE MESSENGER

"The medium is the message." –Marshall McLuhan

1. Here is the first book that taught you women and Indians were just accessories for the protagonist, barely human enough to be proper foils—an old paperback of *How The West Was Won* by that asshole Ronald Regan prototype Louis L'Amour. Also, a rusting pair of Swinger sewing scissors. Take your time.

2. Here is the silver Panasonic radio that announced the war, that first time you ever heard the emergency broadcast system croon its monotone disaster serenade for a lover other than a hurricane. Here is a framing hammer.

3. Here is the billboard on the side of a high rise that promised you cigarettes would make you stronger, wanted. Here is an 8.6 earthquake.

4. Here is the television set that trained your entire generation to sit still and watch. Here is an ax.

5. Here is the pamphlet handed to you by eager Christians with mullets trying to rack up saved souls like Camel dollars; the one that told you any deviation from the body of Christ, any instinct to buck the existence-authorities would land you in hell, permanently. Here is a box of matches that say (appropriately, we think) *Merci.*

6. Here is the old biplane, a Dehavilland Tiger Moth we believe, responsible for writing, "Will you marry me Holly?" in the sky that Saturday at the water, the day you realized he didn't really love you and never would. Here is an M26 hand grenade.

7. Here is the painting that made your heart want, that opened the door a crack to the humming pulsing pulling room of the possible. Here is one hundred years of harsh sunlight and excessive humidity.

8. Here is the letter your father wrote and mailed you, before he tried to kill himself. Here is a brass locket big enough to contain its folded legs. Here is an ocean.

9. Here is the song that forced itself down your throat when you were at your weakest, that wrote you all wrong. It still throbs in you, an alarm clock grinding its gears when the dark rings. Here is your voice.

WHAT COMES AFTER

All night I had been drinking the edges of your face away
with an old friend whose cola eyes could spark wet matchsticks
and who still laughed with her entire body,
even though she had just discovered her husband neck deep
in the stiff ruffled panties of her 22-year-old nanny.

We were both broken and stinging
in that way that trust with it's stuck blade
will turn and cut you open without your permission.

So we drank
until we were righteous and gorgeous again.
We drank until we spilled our guts
like we were subsidized gut factories.
We drank until our metaphors got fat and ridiculous
and toppled over themselves,
and we could no longer agree
whether the war on women had had its Hiroshima
or whether the test or the tost in testosterone
turned men into weapons.

I got so belligerent on this point
that the Goth girl bartender at the punk bar
had to ask *me* to "settle down."
>   *Screw you Bettie Whatever!*
>   *Here's my number.*
>   *Call me when your finished fashioning chopsticks from eyebrows.*
>   *Call me when you're finished sewing Dear John letters to your bed sheets.*
>   *Call me when your angst has expanded to outer space,*
>   *and you're piloting your hopelessmobile to hell,*
at which point I fell off the barstool.

Our money having lost its cashiness at that particular bar
we sat on the roof of her parked car
scheming for more booze and watching
the 2am women's liberation parade
stumble past us in miniskirts and purple lingerie,
purposefully torn tee shirts with girly power slogans,

all clambering after lanky blonde boys bruised from bar fights—
the kind of cheap display of irony from all of us
that makes you sympathize with burqas.
Or want to burn your Victoria's Secret bra
on the doorstep of the local strip joint,
even if you loved that bra,
even if you loved bras in general,
which is precisely what would happen later
after we'd found and finished another bottle of rum.

Hey, she asked, in a voice reserved for lovers high on worship,
you want to see my scar? and pulled the waist of her jeans down
to show me where her daughter had been cut out of her.
I traced the smooth crescent of raised skin with my fingers reverently.
She began humming a tune I had never heard before.
It sounded like a love song to mangoes and butcher knives.
Like a hymn for daughters and rebels and killer wives.

I don't know how we made it home.

When we found my doorstep,
we were laughing so hard the quiet night frowned.
We could barely stand,
so we rested our foreheads together in praise of gravity.
I swear I could feel the dawning of something—
what comes after bitterness,
low in the stomach like sick bees.
I could feel the soft thing that replaces it,
that makes a body ask for forgiveness
by turning slowly to the song.

IF YOUR UTERUS RUNS ON BIRTH CONTROL STANDARD TIME, ALLOW ME TO JOG YOUR MEMORY

It is truly something, after all these years,
how it never fails to catch me by surprise, at least a little,
despite the week of warning signs,
the swollen sore breasts sulking in the cage of an underwire,
the awesome overreaction parade.

How it casts the previous three days in a radical new light—
explaining the asshole on Friday who spoke four decibels too loud
and wore his ego like a unitard of burrs;
why I struggled not to cry when that text message took that tone with me;
why I drank way too much at the Neil Diamond impersonator concert
and kissed that girl full on the flower;
why I ate shit biking home the next day;
why I laid on the couch for hours and hours watching movie previews
and eating chocolate popsicles and feeling sorry for myself;
why I grew forests wanting you to come back.

Slightly dazed at the small rosy sunset of evidence,
I tilt my head to the side and relive it all,
letting the humiliation do its humble work.

I am suddenly not unraveling, sweetwonderfuljesus.
I am not a crazy person, trapped in a spiraling universe
of increasingly implacable darkness and despair.
I am not losing it at all,
or I am, but in the most familiar unchangeable way.
It's just the goodbye party I am never invited to but always throwing.

Just the unwinding of the world's oldest clock,
the one that will wake me up two weeks from now
in the dark first hours of the morning
with its soft insistent ticking.

RADIOACTIVE DATE

After a super sweet woman in Honolulu said to me, "I see things, like auras. It's a gift. And you have a big bright light glowing around you, I have to tell you. I hope it doesn't make you uncomfortable."

No, no it doesn't.
I've always suspected it,
that I'm some clumsy bear of light,
glowing when I think I'm blushing,
burning when I think I'm stealth-ing—
that my aura is bullying the other auras.

I'm worse than a cop with a flashlight; I apologize.
It's a general lack of discipline on my part.
I hope it doesn't make you uncomfortable,
all this unasked-for blazing.
Every time I think I'm finally being cool,
I blunder radiance.
I transform everything
everyone has hidden
so carefully in the shadows
into vulgar electric accessories,
into loud neon chest signs
that say *VULNERABLE!* or *ASHAMED!* or *AFRAID!*

It would be better to leave all that subtext alone,
I know. But we are who we are.
You, with the deep eyes and possible brain tumor.
Me, with the leaking sunshine,
all up in everyone's business with my unchecked fire,
with my incontinent soul.

IS THAT A BIRD IN YOUR PANTS OR ARE YOU JUST HAPPY?

for R.T.

After you poured everything you had
into erotic falconry and inventing languages
for people too lazy to invent their own.

After you communed with the rats
in their nests of wires and absorbed
the Chinese wisdom of no-fucking-way.

After you had your chakras professionally cleaned
by a woman with golden eyes and breath
like bleach and honey.

You no longer knew what to know.
You no longer cared about the knowing part
of the knowing. But you missed the focus—

the eyebrow martial arts with the horizon
of your own abilities! That strain in your chest!
Your inner quitter and your inner show-off

tango-ing and cursing each other out and then
Kablowie! The perfect gymnastic fuck you!
The rockslide love-making! The achieving

and humming along of it all and the soreness
and the proof in your heaviness and the proof
in your wanting it and damn, you really did

all those things they said you did. Thank God
you also mastered the ancient art of not-giving-a-shit
in your free time. It comes in handy doesn't it?

When all that's left is a really good shot of Tequila.
When all that's left is the world biting at your tongue
while you smile and smile and smile.

PLEASE SEND INSTRUCTIONS ON HOW YOU DID THAT

With the sure hands of twelve surgeons,
the quiet need of outlaws with siphons,
the swift religion of hydrogen—
you locked in.
You made branches from my skirts.
You made poems from my alarm codes.
You made little white desserts from my lies.
With no one to observe the tree of my resolve,
the forest of my reasons,
my axes stopped their grinding.
I fell without making a sound.

EAVESDROPPING ON CONVERSATIONS IN LANGUAGES YOU DON'T UNDERSTAND: A PERSONAL ETIQUETTE GUIDE

Proximity

The appropriate distance is the internationally agreed upon 2.5 meters or approximately 4.6 American arm-lengths.

Attire

Some kind of noir sunglasses and possibly a lowered fedora are suggested.

A recent consensus suggests that trench coats are creepy 94% of the time. Except when it's raining, in which case an open umbrella will do.

Body Language

The doing-something-with-the-hands is common courtesy. Try jiggling pocketed car keys or scrolling through porn on your cell phone.

As a final nod to civility, you should crane your neck towards the bus or taxi that's not coming, not ever.

Additional Notes On Style

If the conversation is worth overhearing they won't notice you anyway. Get close enough to really hear what they're saying—the hushed confessions, the warning cadence, the hostile baiting. The I'm-in-love-with-your-wife's, the I-hate-your-guts', the you-will-never-understand's.

Close your eyes behind your shades and pretend they are talking about God and all the other mysteries that skirt your grasp. Pretend they're sharing her most intimate secrets, like where she sleeps at night, and where she got the idea for all those stars. The words are a thousand empty silver screens.

Pull your lips into a serene smile like you've just been let in to the club that all the clubs want to join. Like you just overheard the one thing that will save your life.

THE CONNECTION BETWEEN GOD AND NATURE BEATS ME OVER THE HEAD WITH ITS EARTHY MALLET

I woke up an atheist today
and it is definitely connected
to the lunar calendar pinned by my kitchen window,
its daylights punched out with black x's
marking the nights I've gone without stars.

The Long Beach sunsets are trying to help.
They are massaging my temples with their melted romance,
calming me down with the blood pressure medication
of their mellow collisions with the sky.

Thanks guys.
But I could really use some starlight.
The unadulterated kind.
The canopy of brash burning asterisks
illuminating the vast deep.
My back crashing its shares of gravity to the earth.
My entire field of vision a complex astronomy,
the universe glittering its jewelry,
my mouth hung open like a starving fish—

                            hooked—
breathing shallow in the cold damp midnight.

This is day 3,042 of my inner struggle with city life.
I am staring dreamily out the kitchen window,
watching sun light smelt and sweat in the steam from a cup of tea.
I am picturing myself *ranching*, if that's even a verb.

Later, I will pause under the arches of my 1920s apartment,
survey the teaming broken bookshelves and cockeyed couches,
and fantasize about the sexy promise of open space,
like high school girls in farmhouses must fantasize
about being crushed in the wasted pulsing crowds at rock concerts.

This distance from "the land."
It's a sacrifice you make, however temporarily
to live huddled with the other artists and smart alecks;
to go *months* without being called a liberal hippie
by someone who says it like it's a cancer in his mouth.

It's a choice that makes itself for me
every time I am rescued by the warm clotted glow of art galleries;
by the imitation of Django Reinhardt that is really not that bad,
strumming rakishly out of the mood lit punk bar;
by the David Bowie juke-boxing the punchy patrons
at the cheaper bar down the street.

In the absence of starlight
you start looking for the shine in everything:
        the sparkle of fresh paved asphalt.
        The glinting litter of crinkled candy wrappers.
        The gold fillings in a smile so big you could live in it.
With no forest of trees for comparison,
the smallest signs of life are magic.

God refuses to be outdone by the metropolis.

When you are most homesick, inexplicably,
for some place you've never even lived,
an unexpected ocean breeze salts the heavy air,
stirring everything.

It says: your happiness will return to you
like the prodigal son, having spent
your inheritance of expectations extravagantly,
but ready now to do the work of joy.
Have faith.

The signs of life gather themselves in any darkness.
It's a rebirth, a rebuilding, of what was never really destroyed.
In what is its own kind of starlight,
a thousand bright minds flicker on,
our imaginations like flashlights,
searching for a path,
blinking in the dark.

MY SHITTY APARTMENT KITCHEN: THE HOLY SANCTUARY

Two coats of *Summer Shone Gold*
in interior latex semi-gloss
and you won't even notice
the crappy thrift-store-negligee
slapping together of dry wall and mud
that followed the second burst pipe repair.

Some accent curtains in Tiffany blue
and you really don't see the rain-swollen wood frames
of the single-pane kitchen windows,
the ones that don't insulate worth-a-damn
and won't close, not ever,
or at least not without a lullaby, two bribes
and a powerful Russian curse.
Also: shades of blue stimulate your second chakra.
HUGE BONUS.

The roaches hardly ever come out in the daylight.
Plus they're the small German variety.
The roach-killer-Deltamethrin dust sprinkled behind the appliances
looks like a cinnamon accident.

Furthermore, the framed Oingo Boingo "Only A Lad" album cover
above the pseudo-French doors pulls the eye upward,
away from the terracotta tile they didn't bother to seal.
NO BIG DEAL. No one even notices the blackening grout,
who would notice that? If anything,
the dripping faucet is sounding distractingly musical today,
like the tiniest church bells ever, for a religion you really want to join.

As soon as the gas stovetop oven—turned to 400° Fahrenheit
because *you don't pay the gas bill*—warms up the place,
you'll feel like getting up from the kitchen rug
where you've been sitting for an hour now, wrapped in seven throws.
You'll feel like dancing. You'll peel those blankets off like veils.
You'll go NUTS, all hips, all Action Jackson.
You'll make this 50 square feet your bitch.

WHY THE YOGIS HATED US

Spent our meditation-time poorly.
Focused on our breath until we hyperventilated.
Practiced mouth-to-mouth resuscitation during Vespers.
Demonstrated flexibility inappropriately.
Giggled every time someone said anything in Sanskrit.
Riled up the spirit animals and land cats.
Requested vegan meatloaf "without the vegan".
Broke the harmonium in the music yurt belting out a duet to Wild Horses.
Insisted on calling Kundalini "the hots".
Renamed all the yoga positions after disgraced politicians.
Spiked the serenity fountains.
Climaxed at noon.
Rejected enlightenment before it could reject us.
Fashioned leotards out of paper-mâché.
Sat still as stoned Buddhas to let them dry.
Cancelled the moon dance.
Complained about starch itch for days.

DEAR WIND BENEATH MY WINGS
for A.R.T.

Did you ever know that you're my hero?
Do I even need to ask?
The way you're always flying around in your glory cape,
showing off your super powers. Seriously—
like anyone cares that your vagina can speak
seventeen languages and knit broken bones.

It's kind of embarrassing, the way you're always
batting your fancy lashes and ending civil wars; getting
healing-glitter all over the goddamn place when you sneeze.

Listen, *we get it.*
You're ten times better than us.
A few inspiring words from you and cancer magics itself
into lean muscle mass straight from Madonna's biceps.
You got bored one day and invented the gays.
Oprah wants to eat your pussy on national television.
Again.

I just hope when you're done with this whole
saving-the-world-from-itself-just-by-being-really-rad thing
we can go back to the way things used to be,
back when, thanks to you, I flew higher than an eagle,
and we totally made up all those wing-span-size-matters jokes
and laughed for days. Back when your vagina taught
my vagina to speak French.
Back when we ate toast in bed, fuck the crumbs,
and tangled our legs while we slept,
and there was no pressure
to be anything at all.

ZEN OF THE BROKEN

Be broken.
Lie there
on the ground
in the wreckage
until you can feel
all of your new jagged
edges individually.
Notice how much more
surface area there is to you now.
Notice there's a rhythm to the stinging.
It will lead you back to your pulse.
Try to move if you can.
Follow the path the pain takes
when it forks and sharks
through your body.
Focus on your uneven breath.
Try to love way it hitches now,
how each drag of air cuts
through the field of panic.
As your thoughts struggle
to harden into words,
return to your breath.
Pull yourself into sitting
as best you can.
Be tender.
Try speaking.
Grasp the leathery
harness of your voice.
How long have you been crying?
Hum something
your mother taught you.

Anything is fine.
Feel it vibrate in your chest.
That's where your heart is,
still beating,
still wrestling life into you,
still pushing back against the world.

IF YOU FORGOT TO LEAVE A BREADCRUMB TRAIL

1. Wait for Spring. Drive until you find a good size field at the side of the road. Find the flowers that have broken out like a rash across the brush. Anything that embarrasses you with its gushing. Anything shaking fistfuls of sun at the sky. Make your way to the center, crushing as few as possible. Stand still.

2. When you get home, find the last dress you laughed uncontrollably in. Fold it into a tight square, then a tighter triangle. Using the sharpest scissors in the house, cut patterns into the edges. Shake out the lopsided diamonds of fabric like snow.

3. Blueberries. Lots of them.

4. Do the dishes.

5. Write a resume of all your failures. Now make a list of your dream jobs when you were somewhere between nine and eleven. You know what to do.

6. Lack judgment, in general. In specific: take a shot of whatever liquor you broke up with a long time ago. Shudder hard.

7. Arrive at your mind like a tourist. Using crayons, or lipstick, or whatever you have on hand, make a map of all the monuments, the battlefields, the weird museums. Now add the short cuts.

8. Tape a note to your refrigerator that says knowing yourself is the easy part and then remind yourself of this: applying that knowledge to live your life is like trying to manufacture gills out of dreams of swimming. It's not impossible. But you have to wake up.

9. Wake up.

IT'S NATIONAL FALL-MADLY-IN-LOVE-DAY

Also: Blame-Oxytocin-Day,
The-Neighbors-Won't-Mind-Day,
and Lord-Have-Mercy-Week amongst devout believers everywhere.

The amorousness supplies are high!
You can tell by the lipstick on my ankles
I've decided to celebrate in style.
You can see from the milky look in my eyes
I think I'm ready for anything, and it's true—

we are going to party all other holidays into submission.
We've got mountains of ticker tape
shredded from shitty insincere Valentines
and enough cantaloupe flavored jelly bellies
to pelt the Easter Bunny back
to the religious doubt factory it came from.
We've got a soundtrack of trust fall squeals to clink drinks to.

So why can't I get you on the phone?

A new report by the Department of Miseries
claims 8 out of 10 broken hearts are crushed beyond repair.
It's a tune you've been singing all week.
You are every cynic's back up choir.

I know what the world did to you.
I know it's easy to retreat behind the shields of graceful bitterness.
It is hardest thing in the world to tolerate being loved,
and being loved again, like tanning on the surface of the sun.

But you don't know what I know.

That report didn't take into account that
the most resilient parts of ourselves are hidden
in the bomb shelters of each other's eyes.
It didn't take into account the mounting evidence
that joy is an involuntary muscle.

It didn't factor in that this has been the best apocalypse ever.

So I am submitting a counter-report.
I am submitting grandfather clocks, dozens of them,
locked in a dust-clouded room illuminated
with the ill romance of musty curtain light.
An old bent over clockmaker is winding
and freeing the pendulums at different times,
setting loose a klutzy tinkling that sounds like
pyramids of teacups perpetually buckling.

In only two days time the clocks will synchronize.
It's a law of physics— vibratory frequencies in a closed system
seek the path of least resistance. Pendulums will sway in perfect time
and you would never see the thousand lazy changes it took,
just the sudden satisfying lock step.

Everything wants to be bound to everything else.

Lightning charges someone's porch swing night sky.
It leads to two hands clasping electrically
beneath a blanket that will someday smell like home.
Neurotransmitters leap like liquid fish from crystal bowls
so some kid can learn to play the guitar.
He will write the song that will call her back to you.

Our hearts are just muscle fisted clocks,
keeping their own time with this messy sentiment of drumming.
Even the broken ones. Even yours.

So today we will unlock the good chemistry cabinet.
We will make this world shine again
by installing kaleidoscopes in our peripheral vision.
We will assault this entire town with sweet ukulele jams
and beam medicated rainbows from our chests.
We spill out like gutted pirate treasure chests,
like our sorrows had been rubies all along.

Trust will flood you like a baptism,
like a monsoon of yeses.
The magnets beneath my skin will draw the magnets beneath your skin
and we will power kiss on every bridge we can find.
We will reinvent osmosis.

It's already happening—everyone is falling a little in love with everyone else.
We will get so foolish and boozy just knowing this.
We will be shameless, wasteful gazillionaires of lovin', so flush with love
we will throw it all away and make more, and throw it all away again.
We will regret every second of it in the best possible way,
the way any God who has a thing for apples
must have intended it.

ONE MILE PER HOUR
FASTER THAN THE SPEED OF LIGHT
OR
SUCK IT, EINSTEIN

They want us to believe it can't be done.
Just imagining it makes their fuzzy, sciency heads hurt,
makes the formulas shudder like shotgun shacks.
But I could imagine it all day—
    what happens
    after your mass has crushed in on itself,
    when your soul snuffs out.
    Beyond the reach of all light.
    Past all the wisdoms and isms
    and faces like compasses
    calling you home.

    What's left of you—
    the most impossible parts of you.
    Just air vibrating around the thin waist of a string,
    Just the small gathering changes that tell a cloud to form.
    Your whole being concentrated on existing,
    on remembering existing,
    on inventing new words to tell yourself stories with:
    new words for *dark* and *now* and *yes*.

Sitting here
blinking in the sun
sweating it's light out with my soft chemistry,
I am doing the hot molasses work of dreaming.
I discover life so slowly
the time lapse photographs would show only stillness,

and if you watch long enough,
the steady formation of an arrogant smile.

I don't really care what the geniuses say.
I know about chance.
I believe there must be one ambitious photon who made it.
One particle of light that remembered the secrets to charming barriers.
One rogue spark, who, in the opposite of a flash,
found the other side and became the first to break free,
to prove everyone wrong about everything,
to take a leap against the tide of what we know is true,
the price of which is always
never coming back.

DON'T PRETEND YOU DON'T KNOW WHAT TO DO

Like when you walk into a cavernous ballroom the morning after,
and it has been emptied of the party chairs and the table linens
and the Sophias in their dresses and the twenty piece orchestra
playing everybody's song. It's so quiet. The only sound is the
hollow echoing shine of chandeliers and your good shoes squeaking
on the polished marble. You think *this must be what it's like to
stand on a mountain top. All this rarefied space.*

If you don't dance the dance you were born to in that moment,
in that ballroom, arms flung, legs like a car chase, hair tornadoing
and whirlwinding and burning halos of fuckyes into the dustless air,
you might never speak to yourself ever again. But if you do dance,
every door will stand ajar for you in suspended applause.
Every whispered conversation will pick up volume in your presence.
All the wishes that float just on the other side of what's possible
will take their rules off and run.

Let's skinny dip with them at sunrise.
Let's rip open the bored bodice of met expectations.
Let's enter the moment as children and conduct the notes
bursting out of the lingering money ghosts and just shimmy
that music into every goddamn nerve ending in our bodies!
Let's yell and whoop and shriek and embarrass the frescoes
and shed this dead renaissance!

I was a shy girl once, too, and maybe you fern on the Buddha side
of the waterfall. Maybe what glosses your hair back is the yawning
cave inside of you, the one with the dripping water and focused even
breathing and slow absorption of minerals from the flood and ebb
of your emotions. In which case, take a seat in the center of the
dance floor. Or walk back out of the velvet roped rooms you don't

have permission to be in. Close your eyes to the waiting scandal
of the world and just shrink into the moment. Spend the cash
of your smile as conservatively as you want.

Just let me say this—*you are the most elegant ballroom*
I have ever seen. I hope you understand that I would
never forgive myself if I didn't test out the acoustics
with a little Sondheim, with a little whiskey soda;
if I didn't take the gleam in your eyes for a spin.
This is what I was born to do.
It is the opposite of prayer.
I am listening with the soles of my feet.
I am drawing words from the sky.

ACKNOWLEDGEMENTS

I would like to sincerely thank the team of dedicated volunteers at Write Now Poetry Society and the Lightbulb Mouth Radio Hour for making me believe again in the power of poetry and community. You sure know how to shake the doldrums out of a girl.

I would also like to thank David Reiss for his good looks, his patience, his unconditional positive regard, and his mastery of sauces for everything.

"When The Economy Was Booming" first appeared in the collection *Living Dolls* (Ink Pen Mutations Press).

"Your New Girlfriend Is Really Nice" and "How to Get Under My Skin" first appeared in the love poems anthology *Last American Valentine* (Write Bloody).

"Ultra Violet" first appeared in *The Hawaii Women's Journal*.

Versions of "The Connection Between God And Nature Beats Me Over The Head With Its Earthy Mallet" and "One Mile Per Hour Faster Than The Speed Of Light" first appeared in *Black Boot Magazine*.

ABOUT THE AUTHOR

Mindy Nettifee is Pushcart Prize nominated writer and accomplished performance poet. She has competed in five National Poetry Slams, toured hundreds of venues across America and Europe, opened for indie rock acts the Cold War Kids and Meiko, and curated poetry events for the Smithsonian Project, the Visions Voices Festival, GirlFest and more. She is the author of *Sleepyhead Assassins* (Moon Tide Press). She currently co-produces the Drums Inside Your Chest annual poetry concert series (drumsinsideyourchest.com) and is executive director of the nonprofit Write Now Poetry Society, a national organization working to build the audience for great poetry through education, performance, publishing and grant-making (writenowpoets.org). She lives and writes from the foggy shores of Long Beach, California and can be found at www.thecultofmindy.com.

NEW FROM WRITE BLOODY BOOKS

EVERYTHING IS EVERYTHING (2010)
New poems by Cristin O'Keefe Aptowicz

DEAR FUTURE BOYFRIEND (2010)
A Write Bloody reissue of Cristin O'Keefe Aptowicz's first book of poetry

HOT TEEN SLUT (2010)
A Write Bloody reissue of Cristin O'Keefe Aptowicz's second book of poetry about her time writing for porn

WORKING CLASS REPRESENT (2010)
A Write Bloody reissue of Cristin O'Keefe Aptowicz's third book of poetry

OH, TERRIBLE YOUTH (2010)
A Write Bloody reissue of Cristin O'Keefe Aptowicz's fourth book of poetry about her terrible youth

CATACOMB CONFETTI (2010)
New poems by Josh Boyd

THE BONES BELOW (2010)
New poems by Sierra DeMulder

CEREMONY FOR THE CHOKING GHOST (2010)
New poems by Karen Finneyfrock

MILES OF HALLELUJAH (2010)
New poems by Rob "Ratpack Slim" Sturma

RACING HUMMINGBIRDS (2010)
New poems by Jeanann Verlee

YOU BELONG EVERYWHERE (2010)
Road memoir and how-to guide for travelling artists

LEARN THEN BURN (2010)
Anthology of poems for the classroom. Edited by Tim Stafford and Derrick Brown.

OTHER WRITE BLOODY BOOKS

STEVE ABEE, GREAT BALLS OF FLOWERS (2009)
New poems by Steve Abee

SCANDALABRA (2009)
New poetry compilation by Derrick Brown

DON'T SMELL THE FLOSS (2009)
New Short Fiction Pieces By Matty Byloos

THE LAST TIME AS WE ARE (2009)
New poems by Taylor Mali

IN SEARCH OF MIDNIGHT: THE MIKE MCGEE HANDBOOK OF AWESOME (2009)
New poems by Mike McGee

ANIMAL BALLISTICS (2009)
New poems by Sarah Morgan

CAST YOUR EYES LIKE RIVERSTONES INTO THE EXQUISITE DARK (2009)
New poems by Danny Sherrard

SPIKING THE SUCKER PUNCH (2009)
New poems by Robbie Q. Telfer

THE GOOD THINGS ABOUT AMERICA (2009)
An illustrated, un-cynical look at our American Landscape. Various authors.
Edited by Kevin Staniec and Derrick Brown

THE ELEPHANT ENGINE HIGH DIVE REVIVAL (2009)
Anthology

THE CONSTANT VELOCITY OF TRAINS (2008)
New poems by Lea C. Deschenes

HEAVY LEAD BIRDSONG (2008)
New poems by Ryler Dustin

UNCONTROLLED EXPERIMENTS IN FREEDOM (2008)
New poems by Brian Ellis

POLE DANCING TO GOSPEL HYMNS (2008)
Poems by Andrea Gibson

CITY OF INSOMNIA (2008)
New poems by Victor D. Infante

WHAT IT IS, WHAT IT IS (2008)
Graphic Art Prose Concept book by Maust of Cold War Kids and author Paul Maziar

OVER THE ANVIL WE STRETCH (2008)
New poems by Anis Mojgani

NO MORE POEMS ABOUT THE MOON (2008)
NON-Moon poems by Michael Roberts

JUNKYARD GHOST REVIVAL (2008)
with Andrea Gibson, Buddy Wakefield, Anis Mojgani, Derrick Brown, Robbie Q, Sonya Renee and Cristin O'Keefe Aptowicz

THE LAST AMERICAN VALENTINE:
ILLUSTRATED POEMS TO SEDUCE AND DESTROY (2008)
24 authors, 12 illustrators team up for a collection of non-sappy love poetry. Edited by Derrick Brown

LETTING MYSELF GO (2007)
Bizarre god comedy & wild prose by Buzzy Enniss

LIVE FOR A LIVING (2007)
New poems by Buddy Wakefield

SOLOMON SPARROWS ELECTRIC WHALE REVIVAL (2007)
Poetry compilation by Buddy Wakefield, Anis Mojgani, Derrick Brown, Dan Leamen & Mike McGee

I LOVE YOU IS BACK (2006)
Poetry compilation (2004-2006) by Derrick Brown

BORN IN THE YEAR OF THE BUTTERFLY KNIFE (2004)
Poetry anthology, 1994-2004 by Derrick Brown

SOME THEY CAN'T CONTAIN (2004)
Classic poetry compilation by Buddy Wakefield

WRITEBLOODY
QUALITY AMERICAN POEMS

WWW.WRITEBLOODY.COM

WRITEBLOODY
QUALITY AMERICAN BOOKS

PULL YOUR BOOKS UP BY THEIR BOOTSTRAPS

Write Bloody Publishing distributes and promotes great books of fiction, poetry and art every year. We are an independent press dedicated to quality literature and book design, with an office in Long Beach, CA.

Our employees are authors and artists so we call ourselves a family. Our design team comes from all over America: modern painters, photographers and rock album designers create book covers we're proud to be judged by.

We publish and promote 8-12 tour-savvy authors per year. We are grass-roots, D.I.Y., bootstrap believers. Pull up a good book and join the family. Support independent authors, artists and presses.

Visit us online:
writebloody.com